A Guide to God

For Farmers and Ranchers

SAVANNAH HINKLE

WESTBOW
PRESS®
A DIVISION OF THOMAS NELSON
& ZONDERVAN

Copyright © 2019 Savannah Hinkle.

All rights reserved. No part of this book may be used or reproduced by any means, graphic, electronic, or mechanical, including photocopying, recording, taping or by any information storage retrieval system without the written permission of the author except in the case of brief quotations embodied in critical articles and reviews.

WestBow Press books may be ordered through booksellers or by contacting:

WestBow Press
A Division of Thomas Nelson & Zondervan
1663 Liberty Drive
Bloomington, IN 47403
www.westbowpress.com
1 (866) 928-1240

Because of the dynamic nature of the Internet, any web addresses or links contained in this book may have changed since publication and may no longer be valid. The views expressed in this work are solely those of the author and do not necessarily reflect the views of the publisher, and the publisher hereby disclaims any responsibility for them.

Any people depicted in stock imagery provided by Getty Images are models, and such images are being used for illustrative purposes only.
Certain stock imagery © Getty Images.

Scripture quotations marked HCSB have been taken from the Christian Standard Bible®, Copyright © 2017 by Holman Bible Publishers. Used by permission. Christian Standard Bible® and CSB® are federally registered trademarks of Holman Bible Publishers.

ISBN: 978-1-9736-7365-1 (sc)
ISBN: 978-1-9736-7364-4 (e)

Print information available on the last page.

WestBow Press rev. date: 09/09/2019

This book is dedicated to my family, because they always support me in whatever I am pursuing.

Dear Reader,

Through this book I talk a lot about what God has done for us, how He has made us stewards of the land and animals that we care for, and what that means. I wrote these devotions because I wanted to be able to combine the two things I love most, God and farming/ranching. As farmers and ranchers, we have an undeniable purpose to care for God's creations and I believe that is one of the best occupations someone could ask for. I believe God put us here on this earth for a reason, and we should not take lightly in finding out what that reason is. My hope for this devotional book is to encourage other farmers and ranchers, to show them they're not alone with many of these struggles and share God's love with others. Most importantly you do not have to be a farmer or a rancher to read this book, or even enjoy this book. God's children all have something in common, HIM, and if our career choices and hobbies are not the same, well that is just what makes the world go round. I hope you all enjoy this short book of devotions and get something from it, maybe pass on a verse you got from it too!

In Christ's Love,
Savannah

Contents

Devotion 1	What We Say	1
Devotion 2	Everything is in His Hand	3
Devotion 3	Casting Your Cares	5
Devotion 4	Don't Worry, Pray	7
Devotion 5	In All You Do Serve God	11
Devotion 6	Are You Thankful?	13
Devotion 7	Women of the Lord and Land	17
Devotion 8	Even if You're Young	20
Devotion 9	Blessings from God	24
Devotion 10	We Can do Better	26
Devotion 11	Prayer and Thanksgiving	29
Devotion 12	Reaping What You Sow	32
Devotion 13	God is our Shepherd	34
Devotion 14	Jesus is the Light	36
Devotion 15	The Golden Rule	40
Devotion 16	Your Work Isn't in Vain	42
Devotion 17	Prepare for the Future	46
Devotion 18	God's Timing	49
Devotion 19	Let Go and Let God	53
Devotion 20	Patience	56
Devotion 21	Let God "Rein" Your Life	58
Devotion 22	Count it Joy	62
Devotion 23	Be Not of This World	65
Devotion 24	He's Prepared us a Place	68
Devotion 25	The Road is Narrow	71
Devotion 26	Resisting Temptations	75
Devotion 27	Frustration	78

Devotion 28	He Gives Us Strength	82
Devotion 29	Honor the Lord's Day	85
Devotion 30	He Rescues Us	88
Devotion 31	He Knows Our Path	92
Devotion 32	He Watches Over Us	94
Devotion 33	Joy Comes from God	96
Devotion 34	He Will Provide	99
Devotion 35	Be Joyful, Not Jealous	101
Conclusion		105
About the Writer		107

Devotion 1

What We Say

As most people know, a good three or four days in a row of sunshine in the summer is perfect weather to get some hay cut, cured, and baled. While baling our hay this past summer, our square baler, which is not new by any means at all, stopped tying the bales correctly. The knotter messed up and would not cut the string for the knot to slip off where it is tied. If you know anything about that, then you know it causes the string to snap and break under the immense pressure, which in this instance caused the bale to not have one of its sides of string tied. So, we started looking at the baler, and I said, "It looks like the knife is missing the whole string when it tries to cut." We took it apart and removed ONE washer, just one washer, and it worked perfectly the rest of the day for us. As I was thinking about it, I thought such a small part of the baler was messing up everything for us, but when we removed it, the baler worked great. I was then reminded of a passage in the Bible saying our tongues are a small part of our bodies but can boast great things. Our tongues are just a small part of our bodies, but they can make a huge impact and cause us the biggest mess ups in life! If we remove the bad things that our tongue can produce, just like the washer that was removed from the baler, we can work efficiently and won't cause havoc in our own lives.

So too, though the tongue is a small part of the body, it boasts great things. Consider how large a forest a small fire ignites.

James 3:5 (HCSB)

Devotion 2

Everything is in His Hand

Calving season- it can be one of the greatest times on a ranch and then one of the worst as well. When a brand-new calf hits the ground and stands up to start sucking, well that's probably one of the greatest days a rancher can have. A new healthy calf means a lot of things for a ranch. A new little calf means new life for the ranch, growth and expansion of the herd, and profit from the labor you've put into your livestock. For just a little bit while you watch the new calf getting milk from momma, all the cares and worries of life such as bills, sick animals, weather, or even family issues just subside for a little while; your thoughts go toward this new calf that has been eagerly waited on, and hopes for a good future outcome with it. For a rancher, bringing new life into this world and keeping it healthy is one of the greatest opportunities that is given to us by God. He has entrusted us with His creations. When I think of a new calf that is born or any new creature put on this earth, be it a new baby, new calf, or even a puppy, it reminds me that God is in ALL things. He is the ultimate creator and knows every care we have. God knows about the bills and the payments. He knows that sometimes we're not sure if one of our animals is going to make it despite everything we have tried to get it to feel better. But, God also says He watches over us, loves us, and cares for us like no one else ever can!

The life of every living thing is in His hand, as well as the breath of all mankind.

Job 12:10 (HCSB)

Look at the birds of the sky: They don't sow or reap or gather into barns, yet your heavenly Father feeds them. Aren't you worth more than they?

Matthew 6:26 (HCSB)

Devotion 3

Casting Your Cares

During hay season and harvest season I think I can speak for many individuals, myself included, in saying we have about 1,000 different things on our minds that we are trying to keep up with. Does the tractor have fresh oil? Is the moisture too high? Is it going to rain us out? How many teeth am I going to need to replace on the rake? Will I make the projected yield? These are just a few of the many of questions, thoughts, and concerns that are rolling through our minds as farmers and ranchers during hay and harvest season. Sometimes we let this build up until we burst, often getting mad at those that we love the most, because farming and ranching is a family business. When we feel the weight of the world is on our shoulders during this time, I think the best thing to do is take it to God. Let the One who is always there lift the burden off your shoulders. We're always going to have times we get mad at our closest friends and family members; it happens, we're human. But, during stressful times start talking to God, and He will help you get through whatever you may be going through. God is going to be there when the parts store is closed, and you need just one part to finish up a few more acres for that day. God is going to be there when you must make a huge decision that could affect the livelihood of your family. God is going to be there for you because He cares for you. Just trust Him to help you through.

Casting all your care on Him, because He care for you.

1 Peter 5:7 (HCSB)

Devotion 4

Don't Worry, Pray

A few years ago, my brother and I were moving some of our cows to a new field. We had new calves in with this herd, so we decided to do a sweep of the field to make sure we were not separating a momma from her baby. Nevertheless, my brother found a calf lying in the tall grass that we had missed; I told him not to scare it and be cautious when getting it up because a lone calf will go crazy. I bet you know where I am going with this. My brother got the calf up and got too close for the calf's comfort, so the calf took off running as fast as it could, in the wrong direction of the rest of the herd, of course! The calf went straight for our fence and found a hole that we didn't even realize was there because the calves are usually good at that. They'll find the smallest little place and work their way through if they want out or are curious enough of what's on the other side. Anyway, the calf started running down the road, and I got a little upset and was not sure what we should do. Knowing that chasing it would make matters worse, I thought if we could at least get around the calf and turn it in the right direction that could help. My brother and I, after working for about two hours until it started quickly getting dark, decided to head home and hope the calf would find its way back to its mother. I went home with the calf on my mind all evening, and I prayed I don't know how many times about it. The next morning, I went back to the field to ensure the calf got back in, and sure enough, he had found his way back. I was glad for that answered prayer but made sure to fix that hole in the fence for fear of future issues. I think back on this and even though what happened had me worried I turned it to God and hoped for the best.

Don't worry about anything, but in everything, through prayer and petition with thanksgiving, let your requests be made known to God.

Philippians 4:7 (HCSB)

Devotion 5

In All You Do Serve God

So many people in today's society are against farmers and ranchers because they think we are "pumping hormones" into animals or making "bad decisions" on how we are growing crops or raising our animals. We must keep going and do the best we can, despite the harsh words that are often spoken about what we are doing. What we must do is educate individuals on what we are doing and how it benefits and does not harm others. Everything we do whether it is raising cattle, growing crops, planting crops, harvesting, or feeding and caring for animals, we MUST do it to the best of our abilities, and be honest with those who question us. As a Christian and a lover of God, if I do not do everything to the best of my abilities and try to bring glory to God while doing it, then I am not putting forth the best witness that I could. If we are Christian farmers or ranchers and someone asks how we produce the products we sell, and we are either ashamed to tell them or belittle them for asking, we are not being kind, which is something we are called to do, and we are not doing it for the Lord. In everything we do, we should do it for God.

Whatever you do, do it enthusiastically, as something done for the Lord and not for men, knowing that you will receive the reward of an inheritance from the Lord. You serve the Lord Christ.

Colossians 3:23-24 (HCSB)

Devotion 6

Are You Thankful?

Our culture has taught us to be thankful, especially if you have grown up in church. As a kid, whether you were brought up in church or not, chances are good that you were taught by your parents to say please and especially say THANK YOU, when someone did something for you or gave you something. In Sunday school a few weeks ago, we had a lesson about expressing our thankfulness to God for what He has done for us and our families. As farmers and ranchers, we often forget that despite the countless hours of work, time, and thought we put into our land, livestock, and equipment, it is still all because of the Lord that we have all that we do. Today, the holiday Thanksgiving is supposed to be a time where we stop and think about all that we have to be thankful for, but, it too is getting covered up by the boom of Black Friday shopping that is increasingly taking over Thanksgiving and everything that it means. Families need that time to get together, and as overrated as it may sound, they need that time to just be thankful for what they have and what the Lord has blessed them with. For farmers and ranchers, we have a lot of different things we can thank the Lord for EVERYDAY, not just Thanksgiving. We can thank Him for good health for ourselves, just for waking up in the morning, the sun shining, that it rained, and health for our families and our livestock. If you take into account that God has blessed you so much with everything that you have and start to think of everything you have as a blessing, then life begins to take on a different look for you. Suddenly you don't need to keep getting bigger and better things, and you can freely give to someone in need. I am reminded of a quote I have heard that says what you are taking for granted someone else is praying for. I think this quote is something we need to keep in mind at all times because of the truth that it holds!

When you eat and are full, you will praise the Lord your God for the good land He has given you.

Deuteronomy 8:10 (HCSB)

Devotion 7
Women of the Lord and Land

This is for the female farmers and ranchers or the wives of those in that profession. As a female in the agriculture industry it can sometimes be miserable to try to get the respect you deserve from others in the same field of work as you. The men will always be skeptical when they see a lady walk into the sale barn ready to buy, I'm sure of that. But, don't be discouraged! Take this as an opportunity to learn from this experience and show the men that women can be a very valuable asset to an agriculture company. Ladies on the farm or ranch are very unique because they have to be able to dress up, fix their hair, put on their makeup; and then go assist in a birth of a newborn calf or put in a ten or twelve hour day in the field. Agriculture women must be able to adapt! Some qualities and characteristics that a woman in the ag field, be it ranching or farming, should strive for can be found in Proverbs 31! The verses in Proverbs 31 outline several attributes such as, love, strength, trustworthiness, dependability, and honor. In verse 25 the Bible says, "she can laugh at the time to come." As a woman involved in agriculture sometimes the best medicine is laughter. When so many things have gone wrong in a day, just let it out in laughter. Women have the heart to sit and nurse a sick animal back to health for days and the strength to get up morning after morning to go check a heifer that is due with her first calf anytime. Women farmers and ranchers are so unique and such gems in the industry!

Charm is deceptive and beauty is fleeting, but a woman who fears the Lord will be praised. Give her the reward of her labor, and let her works praise her at the city gates.

Proverbs 31:30-31 (HCSB)

Devotion 8

Even if You're Young

I got my start on a herd of my own when I was young, just before I started FFA, when my parents gave me a heifer we raised. Most of you probably know what that organization is, but if you don't, it is a youth organization that is generally participated in throughout high school. Most students in the program have a Supervised Agricultural Experience (SAE), and mine was cattle. The organization has become very near to my heart, and I learned so much throughout it. Everyone must start somewhere in the farming or ranching business. For those of you who are just starting out, it takes time. You will get through, and do not lose sight of why you started this business. The Lord has perfect timing and there is a PERFECT time for everything. I know right now you may have put just about everything you have on the line and you are probably thinking I may not make this money back; I may not even be able to break even. In the agriculture industry there are good years and, yes, there are bad years. Sometimes, the prices are high and that is just as exciting as Christmas morning when you are 10 years old, and sometimes the market is so low you don't even know if it is worth selling. But, know that the Lord is watching over you and He is with you always. God has a plan for you, and you may not understand it because you see just a few days, but God sees the whole timeline. You, Christian, will come out on top. Maybe not in this earthly life, but if you have a personal relationship with the Lord, then when this life is over and our earthly possessions are all gone, none of that will matter because we are going to be rejoicing with the Lord in a much better place than we could ever imagine. So, if today something is worrying you, or you don't understand why something is happening, remember that there is a time and a season for everything to happen, and if it is God's will to happen, it will.

There is an occasion for everything, and a time for every activity under heaven:

Ecclesiastes 3:1 (HCSB)

For further encouragement read Ecclesiastes 3:1-8!

Devotion 9

Blessings from God

There is something to be said about the many blessings that God shows us and gives to us. Especially the kind of life that we as "off the grid" people live. I can't entirely say that I speak for everyone, but I feel that farmers and ranchers share similar thoughts on blessings. I count it a blessing from God to be able to wake up in the morning hearing cows bawling, seeing the sun shining, and having a beautiful view of fields, instead of waking up to horns honking or traffic noise outside my window. I count it a blessing every time I see a calf born, we finish up baling a field of hay (without any breakdowns), or even when an animal that had a small thing like a limp and we have doctored it and the animal shows progress. I count it a blessing to see what has been planted to feed many mouths is growing and prospering. I count them all blessings because God allowed those things to happen. Each day God blesses us with something; it is up to us to know or figure out what that is. Maybe today you can be a blessing for someone. Hold the door for someone with their hands full, give a compliment to someone that seems down, or offer words of encouragement to a friend that is going through a rough patch. If you look around you, there are many things that can be looked at as a blessing.

For ground that has drunk the rain that has often fallen on it and that produces vegetation useful to those it is cultivated for receives a blessing from God.

Hebrews 6:7 (HCSB)

Devotion 10

We Can do Better

From a farmer/rancher standpoint I can say we are always trying to think about what our next move will be, whether it is financially or operationally. We may be thinking of a new tractor, a new piece of equipment, expanding the herd, or buying more land. Ultimately, we are generally wishing we had more of what we already have. I am not saying that progression in a business and growth is a bad thing, because it is not. But if growth and always trying to be the biggest and best becomes our focus and our sole priority, that's when the trouble begins. We get so caught up in wanting that new tractor because "it'll work so much better," and "get the job done faster," that we lose sight of what should be our main priority, to praise God and bring glory to His name. We are all guilty of this at times, and the devil makes things that seem good take up so much of our time and thoughts that it seems we do not have the time that is needed for prayer, church, or God anymore. The devil hides in things we like to do, and it can become just as bad as committing a sin daily. If we do not remind ourselves to keep the Lord first in everything that we do, we lose sight of why we are doing it. Thinking about this makes me think of a couple verses on priorities, leaving this world, and how to keep God first in our lives. The verses from this devotion show us that we must keep God first and not let our earthly possessions become a first priority in our lives because, in the end, none of that will matter. What will matter is if we can hear the words, "Well done good and faithful slave," from Jesus when we get to Heaven. Matthew 25:21 (HCSB)

For we brought nothing into the world, and we can take nothing out.

> 1 Timothy 6:7 (HCSB)

He must increase, but I must decrease.

> John 3:30 (HCSB)

Devotion 11

Prayer and Thanksgiving

Whether you are a farmer or a rancher, you watch the weather; it's just something you do. When I was a kid and the weather would come on, we were supposed to be quiet so my dad could hear what the forecast was for the next few days, especially if it was during the summer when we were in the middle of hay season. Rain is something that seems to come at odd moments for lack of better words. It seems that when it starts raining it doesn't stop for days, and when it isn't raining, we about get into a drought waiting on it. I have seen summers where we had to feed hay just to get through, and I have seen summers that are green till fall because of all the rainfall. A couple summers ago we were in one of those "dry spells." We hadn't seen rain in a long while and everything was dry and brown in the fields, ponds were getting low, and us farmers and ranchers were getting a little worried. I know we were not in all that bad of a drought, but it was dry, and the situation was not a comfortable one to be in. I started praying and a worship song called "Praise You in this Storm," came to me that I would hum often when I started thinking about the need for rain. Finally, my prayers were answered, and a rain came, and things started looking up for agriculture going into that fall season. Growing up I have learned to thank God when He answers prayers. My dad always thanks God for the sunshine and the rain whichever it may be at the time. So, a prayer of thanksgiving came next, because even though this "Storm," was over for now, I am serving a living God that answers prayers and He deserves praise and thanks for everything He does.

Then He will send rain for your seed that you have sown in the ground, and the food, the produce of the ground, will be rich and plentiful. On that day your cattle will graze in open pastures.

Isaiah 30:23 (HCSB)

Devotion 12

Reaping What You Sow

Too often as people in the agriculture industry our pride gets the best of us and we are not willing to ask for help because we want to know we have it under our own control and are able to take care of everything by ourselves. God wants us to let Him help; God wants us to let Him help in everything we are going through. Time and time again we keep putting trust in only ourselves. Eventually, we are going to fail and need help from the Lord. We as humans cannot handle everything, but God can. God can take your worries and make them seem like nothing, if only you'll let Him. During harvest, hay, farrowing, or even calving season just turn everything over to God and let His will be done, and if you don't like the outcome, it is still part of His great plan. If God is in charge only good will come from it, but when we go about trying to fix something He is doing, we only make a big mess of things. In the book of Galatians, it talks about a man will reap what he sows; if you want to be able to reap the benefits of a good harvest, a good hay season, or an awesome average for your calf-crop then you must be willing to let God help you when you are "sowing." I once heard a pastor say, "God can take your broken pieces and turn them into masterpieces." If that is not one of the truest statements, I don't know what is.

Don't be deceived: God is not mocked. For whatever a man sows he will also reap, because the one who sows to his flesh, will reap corruption from the flesh but the one who sows to the Spirit will reap eternal life from the Spirit.

Galatians 6:7-9 (HCSB)

Devotion 13

God is our Shepherd

Being a good shepherd is important, especially for the animals that the shepherd is watching over. Thankfully for us, we have the absolute best shepherd, God! He watches over us, cares for us, and provides us with our every need. Just like a good shepherd watches over a flock of sheep, God is watching over us as His children. When Satan is trying to tempt us to sin, God is there for us to go to so we can become strong and resist the temptations that Satan offers. If you feel alone, just know God is always there with you and for you, no matter what, and God loves you. A shepherd I would imagine gets pretty attached to his flock after watching over them. In that same way God loves us, He created us, and cares for us and wants to see us succeed and draw closer to Him every day.

The Lord is my shepherd; there is nothing I lack.

Psalm 23:1 (HCSB)

For better understanding and encouragement read all of Psalm 23!

Devotion 14

Jesus is the Light

Going through life without God is like trying to feed cattle in the night without any headlights, difficult. This may be a different way of thinking about a life without God, but it still works. It is the same concept of trying to drive down the highway at night with your headlights turned off; it is not easy, and you will likely get caught in a situation you would rather not be in. Being a Christian in this world is not easy, and nowhere does it say life becomes easier when you become a Christian. Life becomes easier to understand, bear, and keep going through. You learn that what you thought was a huge problem is not so bad after all. We had to feed late one night because of rain lasting so long the few days before then and wanting to keep our hay dry, we waited for the rain to blow over. It was late and dark when we were able to start feeding and without being able to see and not having the best headlights (one didn't even work), it made the job more difficult. I was supposed to be the other headlight when I was on the four-wheeler, and wherever the tractor went, I was to follow. We headed toward the feeders and all the cattle got excited and gathered around, which meant they were right in the way. We were needing to back out to get another bale, so I had to stop being the makeshift headlight to get the cows from out behind the tractor. After an unusually long feeding we were finally finished, and the cows were happy. I thought on the way back, I hope we never do this again! Normally, we would have waited for morning, but it was a Sunday the next day and the cows needed it, so we fed. If we had better headlights on the tractor, feeding at night might not have been such a problem. If we go through life daily walking with God and keep a daily relationship with Him, we might not have as many problems that are so difficult to face. Let God be your headlight.

Then Jesus spoke to them again: "I am the light of the world. Anyone who follows Me will never walk in the darkness but will have the light of life."

John 8:12 (HCSB)

For if anyone considers himself to be something when he is nothing, he deceives himself.

Galatians 6:3 (HCSB)

Devotion 15

The Golden Rule

It seems from the time we are young we are taught "The Golden Rule" of treat others how you would want them to treat you. But, did you know there is a verse that basically says the same thing! In the Bible, in the book of Matthew, Jesus is speaking and says, "Therefore whatever you want others to do for you, do also the same for them-this is the Law and the Prophets (Holman Christian Standard Bible, Matthew 7:12)." When I think about this, I automatically think about helping a neighbor out when he needs it. I feel that the farming and ranching community alike is good at that, but until I had heard this verse, I didn't know that Jesus commands this of us. I think about when a neighbor's equipment breaks down; go either help them fix it, or lend them yours. I remember an older farmer calling us one summer to see if he could cut and bale the hay in one of our fields, and that he would leave us some of the bales. Knowing that we were not planning on cutting the field that year we were happy to let him do that and even got some hay put in one of our barns for us. We didn't really do a whole lot for him, but the older farmer was glad he got some much-needed hay and it helped him out, so we were glad too. Today, think about something you can do for another person and maybe when you're in a time of need you may just get a helping hand back.

Therefore, whatever you want others to do for you, do also the same for them—this is the Law and the Prophets.

Matthew 7:12 (HCSB)

Devotion 16

Your Work Isn't in Vain

As humans, we get discouraged from time to time. We work so hard on something or work hard to accomplish something only to have someone else beat us to the punch or "steal our thunder." The past several years, where I live the feral hogs have gotten increasingly worse, and trapping or hunting doesn't nearly put a scratch on the surface of their population number. The hogs come in a field and in just a few short hours overnight, they have rooted up a large portion of that field. We had just finished discing and reseeding over where the hogs had torn up some land only to see a week or so later, they came in one night and tore it up again. After a while it starts to become discouraging, seeing the mess the hogs make repeatedly. This happens in life with a lot of things we do; we stop seeing the benefit of even trying. Often, we try so hard to always do the right thing and then we start thinking, no one notices; it doesn't really matter, so why not do what is easiest? Sometimes, doing what is right can be more difficult than the opposite. When everything we do seems to go unnoticed, it gets tiresome working so hard for what we see as futile results. But take heart, because everything you are doing is not going unnoticed by your heavenly Father; He sees you and understands the struggles you are going through and wants you to know that He loves you. You have an all-powerful person that can do anything, be anything, and have anything that He wants, but He still wants YOU. God wants you to choose to love Him and accept His free gift of everlasting life. When you become a Christian, you may still get discouraged at times, I know I do. Just like my thoughts of, "what is the point of doing all this work if the hogs are going to just come back and mess it up again?" But that isn't the point though; we as Christians need to keep doing what is right, keep fixing problems, keep doing the "unnoticed" work, because God tells us even when we are discouraged, He is there for us and with us.

Therefore, my dear brothers, be steadfast, immovable, always excelling in the Lord's work, knowing that your labor in the Lord is not in vain.

1 Corinthians 15:58 (HCSB)

Devotion 17

Prepare for the Future

I can't speak for everyone that is a farmer or a rancher, but for the most part I think that we all appreciate and want to take care of the land that provides us with a living. I am blessed that God has given me the opportunity and ultimately entrusted my family and me with a small part of His creation to be a steward of. The land is not only beneficial for our own generation but many to come, so long as we take care of it properly. The generations that come after us can use the land God provides to the best of their abilities if we are doing our part now and taking care of it; sometimes it is hard to undo what has already been done. A verse found in the book of Ecclesiastes says, "What does a man gain for all his efforts that he labors at under the sun? A generation goes and a generation comes, but the earth remains forever." Ecclesiastes 1:3-4 (HCSB) The verses that come before this talk about everything being futile or pointless, so when it asks what is gained from a man's efforts, it is implying nothing is gained because everything is pointless. This verse is not in the context of taking care of the land; it's meaning is that we as humans only have so long on the earth, so make the most of that time; in other words, do not take up your time with pointless things. Live for Christ while you are here, and don't worry so much about earthly possessions because in time they will fade, but God won't fade. He is eternal and a relationship with

Him is the most valuable thing you can have on earth. As farmers and ranchers, we must take the time to be a steward of our land but never forget to take time for our relationship with the Lord.

All things are wearisome; man is unable to speak. The eye is not satisfied by seeing or the ear filled with hearing. What has been is what will be, and what has been done is what will be done; there is nothing new under the sun.

Ecclesiastes 1:1-11 (HCSB)

Devotion 18

God's Timing

I am the type of person who likes to be on time. When I was younger and my family would run late, I would try to hurry us along; my mom would sometimes tell me that maybe God was protecting us from something. At the time I didn't stop to think about it, but it is true. I could only see that wherever we were heading, I was going to have to walk in late and people would know I was not able to make it on time. Thinking back now I realize just how true that statement is. Have you ever heard a story of someone who was late, and it ended up saving his/her life? For instance someone who is normally never late has a flat tire and it causes him to have to change it; only later to find out that if he would have been on time he would have been in the middle of a traffic accident that occurred on his normal route. I can't help but think back to what my mom used to tell me and think it is God protecting me from something. I still do not like to be late, but it doesn't bother me as badly now for that reason.

In the animal side of things, it seems their schedules never match up with mine. When I try to get all the animals worked in time to attend an event, either one won't cooperate causing all of them to misbehave or get worked up. Cattle are notorious for finding a weak place in the fence or a gate that has been left open and needing moved back into the correct field. Usually getting cattle back in is time consuming and wasn't an original plan for that day, so we find ourselves upset that it happened. If we could think that those cattle getting out or the battery being dead in a tractor as protection from God, then maybe when something like that happens, we can smile and just say, "Thank you, God." We may not ever know what He was protecting us from, but whatever the situation is, we should try to be thankful; it could be a blessing in disguise!

But the Lord is faithful; He will strengthen and guard you from the evil one.

2 Thessalonians 3:3 (HCSB)

Devotion 19

Let Go and Let God

Being involved in a business or owning a business means you are always trying to maximize profits anyway possible. Agriculture businesses are no exception to that rule; we are constantly trying to find the cheapest and most effective way to put pounds on a market animal, produce the highest yield, or get fiber products to consumers in a manner that will save us money. We are always trying to do this in a way that will not compromise the quality of our product. If the quantity goes up but quality goes down, it won't be long until word gets around that the product being marketed is no longer what it used to be. This not only hurts a business but the integrity of the business and its future as a producer or marketer. If we turn our business decisions over to the Lord and trust that all is in good hands, everything will work out in the end. I know that can be scary because you feel like you are no longer in control, but I promise you if you say, "Lord, whatever you want with this business, ranch, farm, etc. just let it happen," then you will find peace. As Christians something that is hard to do is simply to obey God because we don't always understand what He is doing, and we don't always understand what the outcome is going to be. But if we start obeying His word and listen to what

He is trying to tell us, then what will come of it will be far greater than anything we could have ever fathomed. If we let go and let God take over our lives and just give it all to Him, and I mean ALL, then God will rain a blessing on us.

A good name is to be chosen over great wealth; favor is better than silver and gold.

Proverbs 22:1 (HCSB)

The Lord will grant you a blessing on your storehouses and on everything you do; He will bless you in the land the Lord you God is giving you.

Deuteronomy 28:8 (HCSB)

Devotion 20

Patience

It was a Sunday in January, not the best time to be waiting on a new calf to be born, but the heifer was already bred when I bought her. For the last week or so I had been watching her very closely. Since this would be her first calf, I was concerned, I went so far as to putting her into a pen to keep an even closer eye on her. I had been doing 1 a.m., morning, and evening checks- basically any time I got a chance, I would go check on her. There's an old saying of a watched pot never boils, and I was beginning to think the same thing about this heifer because she looked like she could pop anytime, but day after day she still hadn't calved. Now, our church starts at 9:30 and I got ready and left. Once I arrived at church, I realized I hadn't checked my heifer right before I left. This worried me but I stayed for services and then went straight home to find that the ONE time I didn't go check on her, she had the calf. She did just fine with her first calf, which made me proud. Waiting on anything in life will teach you patience, but waiting on most livestock to give birth is maybe one of the most tedious waits there is. In life we need to have patience; patience with our friends, family, livestock, and God. Be patient and trust that He will be there for your needs and help you through. Most of the time if we are patient and wait, what is coming our way is better than what we have now. Especially, if patiently waiting involves a new baby, whether it be human or an animal.

The end of a matter is better than its beginning; a patient spirit is better than a proud spirit.

Ecclesiastes 7:8 (HCSB)

Rejoice in hope; be patient in affliction; be persistent in prayer.

Romans 12:12 (HCSB)

Devotion 21

Let God "Rein" Your Life

I teach a class of third graders about once a week on different agriculture topics. I basically explain how they get the food they eat and the products that they use and where it all comes from. It is always cool to see the kids get excited about what they are learning and make a connection that they didn't realize before. One thing I have seen is that some of these kids are not involved with agriculture at all. They have no background in the field whatsoever, but yet they still enjoy learning about and want to get more information about the topics I am teaching on. My biggest fear is being able to answer some of their very well thought out questions that they have! This kind of excitement and wonder reminds me of first becoming a Christian. When you hear the gospel for the first time-or maybe it's the first time it actually clicked after hearing it several times- you start having all these questions that you need answers to. You may not have grown up in a church or have a family that teaches you about the Bible and God's word; none of that may be in your background, but it doesn't matter to God. When we first become a Christian our souls seem to be, "on fire for the Lord," but then as we go through some trials or just life in general, it seems to drag us down a little and we're not that same fired up Christian as when we first accepted Jesus into our hearts. Sometimes we will get the fire back if we attend a Christian concert, conference, church camp, or a church revival. It is always good to get the fire back, but consider this, the bible says to not just be lukewarm. Lukewarm Christians do what is expected of them; they do "JUST ENOUGH," so everyone knows they're a Christian but not too much as to take up too much time. God doesn't want lukewarm, He wants HOT. He wants Christians totally sold out to Him so when they are put into tough situations they choose what is right, they worry about others more than themselves, and they share their faith with others. Will you let God take the reins in your life today?

So, because you are lukewarm, and neither hot nor cold, I am going to vomit you out of My mouth.

Revelation 3:16 (HCSB)

Devotion 22

Count it Joy

It's hard when we're going through life and we all of the sudden seem like we hit a wall. Until we figure out how to get around this wall, we feel "stuck." That wall can be anything for anyone. We all have different weaknesses; some can seem a lot worse because that person may not be able to handle it and some trials may seem like nothing to you but be as big as the world to someone else dealing with the same trial. There are many things that can go wrong on a farm or ranch. Some can happen so fast you don't even have time to think that it was a possible outcome. Struggles in the agricultural life are losing a calf after you have worked with it and doctored it for days thinking it was going to come out of it and losing a part of or all of your crop that you put in so many hours of work to get in the field and growing. No one can tell you how to react when something like this happens; we all carry our burdens a little differently. But God, can ease our pain, and He allowed it to happen to make us stronger when it is over. Many times, we ask why God let something so bad happen when He is supposed to encompass and be the meaning of the word LOVE, but God allows "bad things" to happen because something good can happen from it. We can count it as a blessing, we can count it as a lesson, or we can even count it as joy; but when we start counting the "bad" as something to add to our plate and something we have to keep carrying with us, we start feeling the weight of the world on our shoulders. If we let God help take some of the burden from us and allow Him to make something good out of the mess, whatever it may be, then we can start counting it as joy.

Consider it a great joy, my brothers, whenever you experience various trials, knowing that the testing of your faith produces endurance. But endurance must do its complete work so that you may be mature and complete, lacking nothing.

James 1:2-4 (HCSB)

Devotion 23

Be Not of This World

I believe that farmers and ranchers both know the value of taking care of their livestock and equipment. We realize that when we take care of what we have it will last longer, be there when we need it, and provide for us. Therefore, it is so difficult for farmers and ranchers to see and understand why there are those in our society who are uneducated of the various processes their food goes through and do not trust the food they are eating. Some do not even trust how it has been produced. As agriculturalists we take pride in producing a safe and wholesome product for consumers to buy at the store. We know that if we take care of our livestock, they take care of us. When we sell them, they are likely to bring a better price for us, and if we raise them correctly and a buyer knows this, our profit will go up. It is hard to hear that so many people do not understand that food, especially in the US, is safe and harmless to them; and if it wasn't safe, the food wouldn't be on their plates. As the farmers and ranchers of the world we must not lose sight that we produce these products because we love doing it and it is our job. We must also not get discouraged when we hear stories of people who dislike the agriculture industry and only have negative things to say about it. The best we can do for our industry is when anyone has a question help them understand why a farm or ranch practices certain things with animal health and that it is for overall quality and benefit of the animal. Hopefully when they understand that, they will see the agriculture industry, farmers, and ranchers in a different light. However, when ideas cannot be changed, know that not everyone will always agree with you, and some may even hate you for what you do. For Christians it is very similar. Many people do not like Christians; they call us hypocrites, or even worse. It hurts to hear those names, but just because someone hates who we are does not mean we should change or try to hide our faith. In the same way as when anyone says something negative about the ag industry, we shouldn't try to hide that we are a part of it but rather explain to them why we take care of our animals and equipment the way that we do.

"If the world hates you, understand that it hated Me before it hated you."

John 15:18 (HCSB)

Know well the condition of your flock, and pay attention to your herds,

Proverbs 27:23 (HCSB)

Devotion 24

He's Prepared us a Place

Have you ever had a day that you thought was just perfect? Everything went great and you just enjoyed it? Well, for me some of those days are in hay season. I enjoy working; so, a day of baling hay is fun for me, unless there are breakdowns-that becomes a whole different story when that happens. But a perfect day is getting up and getting everything ready to be out in the field all day and then waiting for the morning dew to dry off the cut hay so that we can start raking and baling it. Then, about noon my family will stop, and my grandma sometimes brings us out some dinner to eat. We all get to eat, talk, and joke a little with everyone before we go back out to finish. To me that is just an overall good day, but I think the best day that is going to happen for not only me, but every Christian is the day we get to enter Heaven and God's Kingdom. The day we get called home is going to be what I call the perfect day because there will not be any more pain, sorrow, suffering, or worries, and Jesus will be there. I don't know about you, but no more things that I would consider bad will influence me. On top of all that, our Heavenly Father will be there; our Lord and no more pain makes for a perfect day, I believe. Thinking of this perfect day reminds me of the song "What a Day That Will Be." In this song it talks about how great of a day it will be to see Jesus and everything we may encounter when we enter Heaven. So, think about your "perfect" day, and see if it even comes close to being the day we are promised as God's children!

But they now desire a better place— a heavenly one. Therefore God is not ashamed to be called their God, for He has prepared a city for them.

Hebrews 11:16 (HCSB)

Devotion 25

The Road is Narrow

Something I have always found interesting ever since I was little is cow paths. I always thought it was so cool to see that cattle have a certain way they always take, and this small and narrow path they follow, always takes them to "major" places that they go to such as water, a tree for shade, or a feed bunk. These "paths" that all the cattle in the herd follow get very worn as they are traveled several times a day by many animals. When cattle are let into a new pasture, you can quickly tell the path that they have chosen to take because the grass will be beaten down and laid over where they all walk. I have found this interesting because it takes all of the cattle in the herd walking on this path to make it show up the way it does; and I just think it is neat how the cattle will keep to the path and generally not stray from it. This "path" reminds me of the path or road that Jesus talks about in the book of Matthew in more than one way. At first the narrowness of the path makes me think of just how narrow the way is that Jesus describes when he says narrow and difficult is the best road. Secondly, Jesus says the road leads to life, and for the cattle these paths lead to their "lives," because all the paths go to food, water, or shelter which is all needed for them to stay alive! So, when you think of a cow path, think of the narrow road that will lead to a life with Jesus. Know that at times the road will be difficult to travel and you may stumble, you may get let down or disappointed, you may even stray from the road, but pick yourself up, and get back to walking on the narrow road because it is going to lead to a better place. Jesus wants you to stay on the narrow road that leads to Him and life because He loves all His children.

Enter through the narrow gate. For the gate is wide and the road is broad that leads to destruction, and there are many who go through it. How narrow is the gate and difficult the road that leads to life, and few find it.

Matthew 7:13-14 (HCSB)

Devotion 26

Resisting Temptations

Has anyone ever snuck up on you or scared you? It makes you jump and a little nervous for a few minutes. One day my brother and I were fixing some fence and a neighbor of ours whose property line meets ours, came up to the fence and sort of startled us since we had no idea that he was even over there. My brother was the first to raise up from the fence, and when He did, the claw end of the hammer smacked me right in the face. I turned backwards covering my eye with my hand. For a few minutes I just sat there covering my eye with my hand until my brother noticed me and said, "What's wrong? Did I hit you?" I said, "Yes!" so my brother came over and looked at it. Blood was coming down my face so, of course, the only thing we had with us was his hankie. I covered my eye with it until the bleeding slowed down. When my brother looked at my eye, he said the hammer hadn't hit my eye but just a little above; it had hit in line with my eyebrow and missed my eye. It later healed and I barely have a scar there now. We can look back on it and laugh now as a memory. This story of someone sneaking up on us makes me think of how the devil can sneak up on us at times without us realizing it at all. The devil will hide and come out when we least expect him. He hides in things that we enjoy doing and that most of the time are not bad at all. However, when those things take our time away from God, the devil is getting his way because the less time we spend with God, or with Him on our minds, the more time we are spending on something maybe ungodly or sinful and something that the devil approves of. So, whatever you do, just be careful to not let a passion of yours take up so much of your time that God isn't a part of your life anymore because the devil will be there ready to tempt you. But, know that you are not alone in this battle against the devil because your brothers and sisters in Christ are with you in the battle, and when you need reassurance or someone to lean on, ask a fellow Christian for help.

Be serious! Be alert! Your adversary the Devil is prowling around like a roaring lion, looking for anyone he can devour. Resist him and be firm in the faith, knowing that the same sufferings are being experienced by your fellow believers throughout the world.

1 Peter 5:8-9 (HCSB)

Devotion 27

Frustration

In farming and ranching there are so many things that can cause frustration and steal our joy away so very easily. If it's not stealing our joy then whatever it is weighs on our hearts and is constantly in our thoughts, which in turn makes us not able to give our all to what is truly important: our faith in God, our family, and our friends. When something doesn't go our way during the day, such as the tractor breaks down for the 4th time this month, you realize you have a cow that's late to calve, or even a sick animal then often these instances can creep up and slowly become our sole focus and our question starts becoming, "Why me?" I have tried to realize and constantly remind myself that popping tires, throwing a belt, running out of something that's needed, a monitor that's stopped working, blowing a sensor, and so many other things are going to happen as they are part of the agriculture way of life, and I as a Christian cannot let these get me down. I cannot let the frustrating things that occur in life steal my joy and become my focus over God. All the bad things generally seem to come all at once when you're already down; it's like the saying when it rains it pours. Sometimes we think this must be God punishing us or, "What have I done to deserve all of this?" The answer is that how you are choosing to look at it is not the case at all. God loves us and is with us always, no matter what we are going through in life. You see, God sees the whole picture and He knows what's around the corner when we can only see just a small glimpse of what is going on. When you think of everything that is going wrong, try to start thinking of everything that is going right and everything that God has blessed you with. After all He did grant you stewardship over a piece of land that I have no doubt is beautiful! When frustration comes our way in life, count the blessings God has shown.

I am reminded of a verse that talks about God always being with us no matter what we are going through in life and to always count it as joy!

Psalm 13:1-6-
In these verses it shows us encouragement that even when we become anxious, concerned, or defeated we can still trust in God's Love!

Devotion 28

He Gives Us Strength

As agriculturalists one of the biggest things that distracts us from focusing on God is spending our time working on the land. Although working on the land undoubtedly brings us closer to God at times because we can stop and look around, take a breath and realize that He created everything that we see. Nothing with the farm and ranch way of life is ever a certainty, and we are always dependent on the weather for how something is going to turn out. Farming is one of the biggest gambles there is; not knowing what the weather will do in the future is often a concern for farmers. For ranchers it is a little different because even when it rains, animals still require to be fed and when it hasn't rained for what seems like forever, animals still need water to survive. A recent example I can think of is this past year's planting season with the flooding. So much rainwater during the planting season has made it impossible for many farmers to get their crops in on time; some haven't been able to plant at all because their fields are two to three feet under water and sometimes even more! That is devastating for the farmers in those situations because their livelihood and how they feed their families has been put at stake and essentially taken away because of the excess rain that they hadn't planned on. Seed, fertilizer, fuel, and many other items were undoubtedly bought in preparation for planting, and now their fields sit under water. The best thing to do in a situation like that is to give it to God because we do not have any control over the weather, rain, sunshine, or anything with nature; only God has control over that. While writing this I began thinking about all the hurt that someone can go through in a short amount of time, and it doesn't just happen to those of us involved in the agriculture industry. I began thinking about those that have something happen unexpectedly, such as an accident that changes the course of their lives and their families lives forever. When I started thinking about that and connected it to living on the farm and all the things that can go wrong on a working farm and ranch in an instant without realizing it, one verse came to mind, Philippians 4:13. For everything we go through no matter if it is unexpected rain and bad weather, an accident that left someone or yourself in a bad condition, or just a bad day for some reason, we can still go on with life because God is our strength.

I am able to do all things through Him who strengthens me.

Philippians 4:13 (HCSB)

Devotion 29

Honor the Lord's Day

This past Sunday my pastor was preaching a sermon and used these verses: "As obedient children, do not be conformed to the desires of your former ignorance. But as the One who called you is holy, you also are to be holy in all your conduct; for it is written, Be holy because I am holy (Holman Christian Standard Bible, 1 Peter 1:13-15)." As my pastor read these verses, I started thinking about them and what they meant. I thought about everything we read online with social media every day and what some of the desires would be that we are not to be conformed to since we have become a child of God. On social media every day we see SO many things that God lays out in the Bible as wrong are pushed into the spotlight as being acceptable and just fine for people to engage in. "It doesn't matter if you are a Christian and want to do wrong things because God will forgive you," is what social media wants to portray. God will forgive us, but if we truly are a Christian, we shouldn't want to sin and go against what the Bible says in the first place, and if we do slip up and sin, because we all do, we should ask for forgiveness and try to not repeat our mistakes. As Christians we should want to change when we become a born-again believer. On the farm and ranch we may do things differently as well to adjust to that change. There are always things to be done, and generally it seems there is not enough time in the day to fit them all in. That being said, those that struggle with taking time to go to church because of work that needs done or something needs fixed for the upcoming week, I strongly encourage you to take the time to go to church! In your mind you think, "I am just missing one Sunday; it won't hurt." But, one Sunday turns into two and then before you know it, you've missed a month. Nowhere in the Bible does it say we must attend church a certain number of Sundays out of the year, but many times it talks about gathering together with other believers. Take Sunday to be with the Lord, worship Him, and draw closer to Him. Give your land, your animals, and everything you have worked for to God, and let Him have His will with them, because the blessings that will come on you for just giving everything to God is more than anything you could imagine! I understand that there are busy seasons in life, and we go through a rough patch at times, but remembering who made it all possible for us to do what we do is so important.

Not staying away from our worship meetings, as some habitually do, but encouraging each other, and all the more as you see the day drawing.

Hebrews 10:25 (HCSB)

Therefore, with your minds ready for action, be serious and set your hope completely on the grace to be brought to you at the revelation of Jesus Christ. As obedient children, do not be conformed to the desires of your former ignorance. But as the One who called you is holy, you also are to be holy in all your conduct; for it is written, Be holy, because I am holy.

1 Peter 1:13-15 (HCSB)

Devotion 30

He Rescues Us

I have learned that life is all about how you look at it, and the perspective that we choose to take toward what happens to us is often what leads to our attitude and overall happiness. With farming and ranching it is no different at all. It could be the worst day on the farm, but if WE choose to look at it in a positive light then we can figure that something could always be worse, and many people often have it worse off than us. I have some friends who are a couple that I was speaking with, and they were telling me about a pretty rough day they had the prior week. A cow had gotten down and didn't pull through, the skid-steer they were burying it with got overheated several times before it was all over with, and on top of all that my friend's mother had taken a bad fall. After they had told all this, immediately my friend said, "God was watching over us though because we finally did get the cow buried, the skid-steer running, and my mother did not break anything just some minor bruising." This made me think, "Do I praise God even when things are bad for them not being as bad as they could?" I know I do not praise God nearly as often as I should, but when they told the story and had the positive perspective that everything was going to be okay, it encouraged me. Life is sort of like a mud puddle, worrying about something starts off small just like the puddle but then starts weighing on our minds more, just like when you keep driving through the mud puddle making it bigger. Whatever you are worried or stressed out about, if you don't let that go and let God have it, your life can become overtaken by it. The mud or the stress can sometimes become so deep you need help through it so you put it in four-wheel drive and pray to God about it and understand that He is taking care of you and the situation at His timing and not our timing. Only then will you get through the puddle or the rough patch in life.

I found so many verses that deal with giving all you have and whatever is on your mind to God that I picked three!

Call on Me in a day of trouble; I will rescue you, and you will honor Me.

Psalm 50:15 (HCSB)

If I say, "My foot is slipping," Your faithful love will support me, Lord. When I am filled with cares, Your comfort brings me joy.

Psalm 94:18-19 (HCSB)

Don't worry about anything, but in everything, through prayer and petition with thanksgiving, let your requests be made known to God.

Philippians 4:6 (HCSB)

Devotion 31

He Knows Our Path

For the majority of those of us in the farming and ranching community, I have seen we all are willing to help a neighbor and lend a hand. Though we often pile too much on our plates and can't get everything accomplished that we would like to. I remember a time when I was supposed to be to a certain place at a specific time. Well, I was already running a little late because of finishing up things at home, and I tore out headed to town as quick as I could. I didn't make it but a mile past my gravel drive on the highway when my truck started making an odd noise and I had to slow down and pull over. I slowly made my way back home and had to haul my truck into the shop to be fixed. Later I was thinking about that day and thought the Lord has a way of humbling us and protecting us as well. Maybe if I had gotten up the road a little quicker than I had I would have gotten in a wreck and been injured. God humbled me that day in making me realize that I am not in control of my life. In our day-to-day we often get caught up and pile way too much, promising others we will be there for them and help them out with something when sometimes we just need a break. That day when my truck broke down, I still rushed to get where I was going in another vehicle, but thinking back, I realized how lucky I probably was and that my plans aren't always God's plans.

"For I know the plans I have for you" -this is the Lord's declaration- "plans for your welfare, not for disaster, to give you a future and a hope."

Jeremiah 29:11 (HCSB)

Devotion 32

He Watches Over Us

As much as we would like to be, we can't be everywhere all at once. We aren't physically able to be spraying for weeds in one field while planting in another or watching over the livestock at all times of the day and night. We aren't even able to get the work finished around the house and be out in the fields at the same time. But God can be at all places all the time watching over everything. Think about that for a minute. God is watching over you right now; He knows what you're thinking (good or bad). Today and every day we should do things that are pleasing in the eyes of the Lord and keep in our minds that He is always watching over us. Even if we don't feel God, He is there. Too often we think everything needs to be finished all at once and that we have a certain schedule we need to keep up with, and with many things this is true. But, if one thing doesn't get finished in a day, do not be so hard on yourself and make sure to be understanding with your loved ones! So, put your faith in God and your trust in Him and when you can't be in three places at once, know that God is taking those situations into His hand and everything is going to work out.

The eyes of the Lord are everywhere, observing the wicked and the good.

Proverbs 15:3 (HCSB)

Devotion 33

Joy Comes from God

So many people these days are half-in with their faith! I get it, I really do because it is SO hard to be a part of this world and live for God because of the endless amounts of distractions, and sin that continually goes on. Becoming a Christian is the best decision that you can make for your life but one that does not need to be taken lightly. When you first become a Christian, you're on a sort of high for a while in your faith, but then the first bad thing that happens or comes your way, it quickly takes you back a step! But I will tell you this, God is going to be the most constant person there will ever be in your life. If you're looking for consistency, someone who is going to be there for you when no one else will be, then God has never left anyone, and He won't start with you. Whenever someone is in your life leaves or someone moves and contact isn't very constant, you can always talk with God. He will be there day or night and hears you when you are speaking with Him. The Bible has a name for those of us Christians that are "half-in." A lukewarm Christian is when you aren't totally on fire for God. I imagine that most of us get a little lukewarm at times, and we falter, taking a step away from God and our faith, but making sure you catch yourself and get back on track with living for the Lord is a necessity. I have spoken previously about being lukewarm and what that means to God. Making sure we are not lukewarm takes a daily reminder and a constant walk with the Lord. I am as guilty as anyone else to forget to thank God or recognize Him for all that He has provided for my family and me. When I think of lukewarm, I think of the temperature of water. The temperature of water needs to be different depending upon what you are doing. For example, if you are needing to boil something the temperature of water needs to be much hotter than just lukewarm. If you are mixing up a bottle to feed to livestock or a baby, the water cannot be boiling but still should be warmer than lukewarm! So next time you are mixing up a bottle and heating the water remember to not be lukewarm, and that the struggle of continually feeding the animal is worth it! The verses found in Psalms 126 show struggle, hard work, and a good outcome because of the Lord!

Please take the time to read the 6 verses in Psalms 126! I have included one that really outlines just everything God encompasses.

The Lord had done great things for us; we were joyful.

Psalms 126:3 (HCSB)

Devotion 34

He Will Provide

Of all the roads we take in life many of them are dirt and gravel, always bumpy, and often traveled by very few people. For the agriculturalists it seems to be something that we are just used to and don't seem to think all that much about. A friend of mine wrote that life is a lot like a gravel road; the rough patches are the potholes we always seem to hit and the turns and curves that come up are the totally unexpected events that occur in life! She talked about driving down this gravel road called life and not letting the worries of the world and the troubles continue to keep us down because our Heavenly Father cares for us! He has control over our lives and is watching over us while we continue down our road of life. Honestly, God does so much for us, and I think about all the close calls several of my friends and family members have had and I thank God continually for keeping them here with me a little longer. We are all living on borrowed time and never know when we are going to have to give it back, so we must be prepared for eternity. The only way to truly be prepared for eternity is by trusting in God and knowing that He is your Lord and Savior. I know that this is the big message that always comes from Christians, but I think it is important that it is said because you must understand that YOU have to invite Jesus to live in your heart and be the master over your life for you to be changed.

For God loved the world in this way: He gave His One and Only Son, so that everyone who believes in Him will not perish but have eternal life.

John 3:16 (HCSB)

He causes grass to grow for the livestock and provides crops for man to cultivate, producing food from the earth,

Psalm 104:14 (HCSB)

Devotion 35

Be Joyful, Not Jealous

Throughout life we get compared to others often. We compare ourselves to others a lot as well. Usually it ends up not even helping us; it steals our joy, and makes us feel down about ourselves. We seem to continually compare anyways. It may be comparing the way we look, the way we dress, what kind of vehicle we drive, or the house we live in. From an agricultural comparison point of view, I tend to think that what gets compared is a little different from the looks of it, but the idea of comparing just hurting us in the long run is still the same. In the agriculture industry we may compare ourselves to other farmers and ranchers within our community that we know. We may see the tractors, number of animals, acreage or land they own, or equipment they have and think that they have it all and they are so lucky. But we are not to compare ourselves to others, especially when it brings jealousy into our being! It is very easy to get caught up in comparison though and it can quickly takeover all our thoughts if we are not careful. It consumes us and keeps drawing us in, and everything that we think about becomes what others have and what we do not have. Be very mindful in how quickly it can become a part of your life, and remember that you do not always see how everything is working for that individual either. They may have new equipment, a lot of livestock, and new tractors; but they may also be drowning in bills and loans that they have taken out to acquire everything! Remember God takes care of His children in all ways!

Even in laughter a heart may be sad, and joy may end in grief.

Proverbs 14:13 (HCSB)

A tranquil heart is life to the body, but jealousy is rottenness to the bones. Proverbs 14:30 (HCSB)

Study through chapter 14 of Proverbs for further understanding!

Conclusion

A pastor once told me people today don't just want to hear what God did in the Bible, they want to hear what God is doing for you right now in your life. I feel that I have written these devotions as a way to share my faith with others. I am trying to understand the lesson I am supposed to get from different experiences that I go through so that I can tell others about them, and possibly help someone that has similar experiences along the way. With God's help I am being blessed with finding the lesson I was supposed to get from a situation I was put into. I don't really know who or if anyone will get anything from this short book, but if these devotions help just one person it did what it was meant to do. I hope you as the reader get out of this book everything God meant for you to. I know as people that are involved in farming/ranching- or any kind of agriculture, there seems to be a need of a few more hours each day. I also know it is easy to get down because of the hardships and tough times that the agriculture industry is going through. But I feel it is important to realize that we must set aside time for God and attend church regularly to keep our focus on what is right and to remember what is truly important, God. Whatever you do in life, keep the One that holds tomorrow first in your life!

About the Writer

Savannah Hinkle is currently working on a degree at Southeast Missouri State University, majoring in Agricultural Education. She has grown up on the family farm where her family works together to raise beef cattle. Savannah has always loved the farm life and everything that comes along with that lifestyle! She has taken agriculture classes since her freshmen year of high school, and quickly realized she wanted to make a career that was related to the agriculture industry. Although her plan is to never get far from the farm life, she never knows where God will take her. Currently she hopes to obtain an education degree to someday teach agriculture courses at the high school level. Savannah has been blessed to grow up with a family that taught her the importance of church, showed her the right way to live, and has always supported her. Savannah's church family at First

Baptist Church of Fredericktown has been a huge part of her life and has been a great influence on her. Her knowledge and faith have grown tremendously while being involved in her church youth program. Savannah's passion is serving others. She has been blessed to take part on several mission trips to various places and her faith has grown with each trip. Three words that describe Savannah's priorities are: faith, family, and farming; in that order. She enjoys living the simple and rewarding life that God has blessed her with in Missouri!